IMMORTAL
SOFT-SPOKEN

IMMORTAL SOFT-SPOKEN

robert vivian

Immortal Soft-Spoken
© 2018 Robert Vivian

First Edition, 2018

Published by Awst Press
P.O. Box 49163
Austin, TX 78765

awst-press.com
awst@awst-press.org

All rights reserved.
For permission requests, please contact the publisher.

Printed in the United States of America
Distributed by Small Press Distribution

ISBN: 978-0-9971938-6-2
Library of Congress Control Number: 2018933599

Editing by Tatiana Ryckman
Copyediting by Emily Roberts
Book and cover design by LK James

This headlong book is dedicated to the memory of my grandfather Robert Scott Vivian—and to the rivers where I wade and dream, even when I'm nowhere near them.

CONTENT

3	Be My Obscurity
6	Before I Send This to You
9	My Breath in Your Breeze
11	Wild M
14	Come Forth and Enter
17	Little Mouth
19	Sound of Day
21	Echo Moth
24	Every Winter Darkness
26	Glory
29	Ladybug
31	Mouse with Dandelion
33	The Dark Unspoken
35	Candle with Words
37	Skin of Earth
39	Immortal Soft-Spoken
41	The History of Kneeling
43	Another Sky
46	Chanting by Breathing
48	Nebraska Prayer
50	Bird in My Mouth
52	Blue Always
54	Click Here to Begin Your Ascent

56	Poem I've Never Heard Of
59	What Touch I Wonder
62	If I Say Grandfathers
65	Dream Animal
67	Fey Tenderness Once More
69	Dust Mote Deliverance
72	Confessional
74	St. Francis Hearing Traffic in the Garden
77	Maybe Essay
79	Birds to Sing Me
81	Pulse
84	Black Ink Essay
86	Wonder
89	Essay Breathless in a World of Cloud and Smoke
92	God-Husks
94	Last-Minute Contributor
97	Green of Me
100	How the Days

O indigence at the roots of our lives,
how poor is the language of happiness!

> **Osip Mandelstam, "Tristia"**

With the gathering force of an essential thing
realizing itself out of early ground, I faced in
myself a passionate and tenacious longing—to put
away thought forever, and all the trouble it brings,
all but the nearest desire, direct and searching.
To take the trail and not look back.

> **John Haines,** *The Stars, the Snow, the Fire*

All the world began with a yes. One molecule
said yes to another molecule and life was born.

> **Clarice Lispector,** *The Hour of the Star*

Be My Obscurity

I woke with dawn in my mouth and it was spilling all over with birdsong, with flower, with the after moths of thunderstorm and dawn said I'm going to speak you now, I'm going to rev you up to gaga mode and I said okay, use me, wring me out like yon dishrag of much wanting and wantonness and then it was pure vintage moan, the kind that shivers the chandeliers of a woman's clavicles or my dear Hungarian grandmother long into the ground whose smile stretches across the centuries and connects the dots of constellations and waking with dawn slipping out of my mouth I said reckless and miraculous things like I love you, brook trout, I love you, wormholes, I love you obscure book of poems and will you be my obscurity, will you be my chiaroscuro, will you be my almost unknown for it is true a river whispers to me Come hither, come my thread-most and I do, I do with a fly rod in my hand and a two-day stubble and faint after-echoes of hereafter, the misty-eyed kind though I am wrecked and shaken by early-morning awe and this crazy love of words and music that drives me to my knees and puts the Lord in my mouth like dawn, like dawn and every new beginning and the first kiss in second grade when I swear I could almost fly and church was a many-splendored stained-glass kaleidoscope prepping me for a river many years hence which I continue to crawl to on all fours, oh, Lord, I am coming, I am coming, I am and all creation be praised as I am just learning how to truly say Amen, amen as this pen skitters across the page like my own imperfectly tied fly, the one that looks like a broken hobo, the one that looks like a broken rainbow the fish take pity on, love for their own broken sake, rising in brief boil of sacred river, my own heart skating after it like some forsaken prince deep inside my chest who has forgotten his password, his wallet in the very midst of kingdom come and fall down Moses on his knees and thus spake the dandelion and Bathsheba more beautiful and splashing over than any ocean wake and bramble, wildflower, the leaves whirling like dervishes, my own quaking stillness something to take pity on and even adore as one tiny creature in this universe of soundless praise ringing down the home stretch, ringing down forever.

Before I Send This to You

One word out of many and some other stirring of branch and thistle, leaf tremble and quake, the sudden dash and comma, Emily Dickinson in a flash of poetic lightning, oh, must get it down now, must get it placed and said among the miraculous ten thousand things as here this early morning one word, then another, a man playing carefully with textures and tones under an always shifting sky of star and cloud here then gauze-covered and boomerang of moon come back again but one word and then another, the words coming together by themselves like wild animals in deepest and listening woods, the words then breaking apart, the words and how they taste and how they sound, taste-sound sweet and salty on the tongue by way of roof of mouth and pressed against my teeth, all dentition in the service of a cry and how this miracle of breathing must form an utterance and how this utterance carries forward before dawn to no one or to all, and how I am blind in my speaking and blind in this joy as the dictionary waits to be held and consulted, rocked even, waits to be page-driven in a snowstorm and words emboldened, blackened for who is he, is she whose grief and joy bear such an emphasis and regal dignity, book of keen exercise as it makes way and gives sanctuary to one word then another all the days of its tea-sprinkled life and would you marry a dictionary, would you bury it one day like a loved one and through and by which my own life is wedded to a playground of words and how the words are rising even now and you can see them as scattered particles of an intergalactic poem called Here Thy Wind-Riven Night and how I hold and ponder them for meaning, for mysterious delight and how I and the words shiver together this winter morning wondering if we are part of an open book and what page, what sentence, how the life of this is being written on the page by someone who does not know but wonders, wonders, and loves a little too much, the high dive of a colon, the feeling of this page before I send this to you and to beloved Aunt M in Muskegon by holy post by hand and licked envelope and DNA-stained forever, an offering, a seal, a kiss that covers a long distance, a continent, a century, maybe even the smack-dab kiss of forever.

My Breath in Your Breeze

O breeze, breeze, causeway of my name and every name, all breathing, all sighing and light dappling through the green, green trees and my breath in your breeze and late-May coolness before and after heat, breeze I hear and breeze I am and all inspiration and expiration and invisible God deep within and every spirit, every waking and quaking and trembling sound, spirit breeze and restoration of earth and fish rising again in my wide-awake dream and I rise with them each time, each holy and prodigious hatch and then limb I venture out on, limb that I am and this wild verse laced with wild air, wild breathing and breeze that no one owns, possesses, can capture, contain or plastic bottle defacing and disgracing, wild, wild breeze my brother and sister and the covers of a book open to green leaves of poems here I commit my spirit to your ever-shifting wafting that moves and inspires me and the oneness I hear calling all of us, calling me so softly, softer breeze now touching my forehead, my eyelids and my lips in the kiss of a beautiful woman whose body heat radiates the grace of this heartbreaking and heartmaking earth, O breeze almost gone rushing over me, rushing through me in the gentlest caress the world has ever known, featherweight champion of all time in the tender division, weightless and almost winged, giving birth to me, most flawed and imperfect man and drinker of vodka, whispering the words I do, I do at the altar of birdsong and grace, O most splendid and everlasting, most numinous church and the altar of verb where I sway like a candle flame, man-flicker and wobble, grooving where I burn and I turn back to astonished air threading effortlessly through the smallest lattice of branches and trees, skeleton dance and weaving where I barely miss every outstretched tendon, bone, moon shiver, and vine.

Wild M

Please peel me open to inner music once more and say/speak/sing/rock it in tumbling outpouring, to lash out with love and astonishment the headlong carrying away with words so please carry me away, away out of myself, every last stitch and sinew like plucked violin strings in E major, C minor and dear wild M, wild mistress of moan, wild bird whistle and trumpet flower for my throat is aching and dry, empty and raw for the pathway of your spirit to sing again or wail and so willing this morning to be thy humble instrument and servant, hardworking towel boy for the verb to be and I will shine your shoes, wild M, verily with my own foam-flecked spittle though I know you are barefoot and coming just now from the woods after hunting mushrooms and strawberries and wildflowers in your long black/blonde/chestnut-colored hair and what is a man like me but waiting vessel, open wound, accordion player with a monkey on his back and battered tin cup held out from monkey's hand for spare change, spare change, do you have an extra nickel or dime, mister and miss, regal mama and I will sing for my breakfast bar, I will sing for my vodka and sing to be saved from myself who is bound to earth but looking forever skyward/celestial/the holy roaming stars and my singing among their wild turning for I taste the starlight you gave me, precious M, and it tastes like nothing within the boundaries of my raked-over buds—the taste of vastness and distance inconceivable, unspeakable, outside the compass points even of gobsmack, the threadbare center of a drop-away abyss, the taste of the moon and its screeching chalkboard, taste of the ocean, the mystic salt and spray and a fire that burns up my tongue like a lit fuse and every interstellar color as I swallow the world again and again praising it, oh, sing me until I burst into otherworldly and first flower, cottonwood spore drifting in a meadow and the blurring bruise of a hummingbird's wings like small dynamos of winged electricity before sucking the nectar out of every flower with a passion that would drain even the hard-staring countenance of stones to fill the rivers again with rainbow bending water speaking our names as if for the very first time, wild M, wild mustang, wild, wild, wild please take up your torch inside me and wave it around until I fall to my knees in a heap of cascading sparks and poem, your sounds flooding through me, the sighs, the wails and cries of ecstatic release, the whispers in what broken tenderness this is and must be.

Come Forth and Enter

To come to the gate of the world, to enter it bowing and all adoring, the gate miraculously unlocked and no script to follow for entering, no ironclad rules, to walk through the gate of the world naked and trembling, to hear the gate swinging wide and not rusty per se but almost groaning, yes, a groaning gate at the heart of the world, to gently push open the gate and walk through, to hear my own footsteps treading on the ancient trail, to open the gate of the world and know many have passed before with great joy and great sorrow and pain unimaginable, to come finally to the gate of the world, to say Jesus and Rumi, to say St. Francis and The Little Engine That Could, to pause at the gate of the world and hear birds singing in the dark before dawn, to touch and hold the gate before gently pushing it open, to hold the gate in vast threshold of awareness, to somehow know and intuit on a level beyond reason that the gate is made of love and justice, to know its cross-thatch of straw and hoar frost and early morning poems, to realize that the gate is my friend and my mentor, then to lean into the gate with my shoulder, with my everything and whatnot, to come at last to the gate of the world and hear my heart pounding not in fear but deep inner excitement and the memory of every trembling brook trout in my hands, wet hands, the gospel of brook trout and every wormhole of verse and vermiculation, to walk through the gate at last and know that I am being watched by ancestors who suffered more than I will ever know, to hear even the stones ring with gladness as I walk to the center and a breeze touches my face, to enter the gate and not look back, leaving every pillar of salt behind, to know that I am finally home and one with all there is, to know that death is just like stepping into another room with bright windows and glowing rays of starlight, to bless the gate with my passing and to walk in a sacred manner as Black Elk speaks of, to hear a river flowing in the distance beckoning me to follow and to follow this water even as I hear it coursing through my veins, my body, my beating temples as I say thank you, thank you to the journey and the upright carriage of my new body for after the first death it is only life forever, to love as I have never loved before as my breath turns into prayer, a part of the sky, an offering, the frail mist I was created to give.

Little Mouth

Many mouths and many rivers and here a little mouth still speaking, still whispering, univocity of grass and stone and this little mouth raised to the stars, saying great mystery, great wonder and tenderness and windswept snowfall in laces and lashes of drift, perfect dunes, perfect roundness and sculptures of cliff and mouths in these also, small mouths of snow saying cold, cold, clean, clean, and will you marry me on this altar of slope and Yes, I say, yes, I will marry you, little mouth in the vastness of winter silence where the earth lies hushed and listening for spring months away and little mouth and lips parted in wonder, in almost saying and almost sobbing how beautiful it is, the sighs that would heal the world one breath at a time and restore the ozone to grace and I feel my own mouth forming and tasting words of praise and lifting them to the roof of my mouth, little hayloft, little attic space and spelunker of poem and verse and the little mouths everywhere saying yes to light and yes to dawn and bedside flowers opening by the long lane and dying in rooms fathoms away from cartwheels of childhood and cottonwood spores and a church bell tolling in the distance in peals of little mouths singing one sustained O and O the perfect shape of any mouth, O the chasm through which we all plunge not knowing the whys or wherefores, only holy, holy, only falling and how the little mouths will sometimes touch and sometimes merge in a deep-throated kiss or resuscitation and how beautiful and necessary these are, to kiss madly and with this plunge commence all earthly oxygen and no hissing, no cursing, no saying we are not gentle, can we be loving and brave and how our mouths again become circles, become Os, becoming planets and stars as we speak of the light and let it pass through our mouths, our words, our touches and quaklings of sound, eternal freefall beyond time and distance and dreaming, lighter than wing or feather, a song.

Sound of Day

And then the words come to the edge of a field, the words sleek and quiet over the earth, the words turning primitive again, pure sound, *Mmmm* and *Oooo* and *Lalala*, tip of the tongue on the bottom of one's teeth, words making love with tongue and teeth, spoken rush of bodily words no words at all pure sound, pure nonsense, sound of day and sound of awakening, fish a sound and rod, a sound and the oneness they become in dream after dream after dream where I wade in the sacred hunting grounds of bends of river, oxbow, deep pool of stillness and pellucid clarity where I cast and cast and cast again, throwing myself into the ancient ways of listening/looking/stepping alacrity central and every verb used with sacred handling as my very vocation is verb, is movement and on the move, pure sound and listening and who/what/where to guide me but wind and trees and water as I become pure animal once more, a living pulse of dynamic ache, floating line and woolly bugger, parachute Adams, myself a rooster, a hackle, drinker of vodka and far-gone lover of women's bodies, their shapes, their hourglass figures and smiles and high-up laughter and the poem I recite in the dark about holding hands, a kiss, then water, water, water again and clear forever, rising fish and fish that know me better than I know myself, fish teachers, prophets and poets, fish maestros and iridescent scales, vermiculations and wormholes, holy universe and temple of breathing water in and out of the shallows, the depths, how I keep returning to you again and again and again for us to catch each other, to suffer together in agony and ecstasy even as I cut off your head and disembowel you, even as I eat your raw beating heart as the sun goes down as one day you will eat mine, blood brother and sister, stalker of mice and spiders and thunderstorms, grasshoppers and sky above Michigan, the first light of morning and mist rising from the river, prayer that never ends, prayer that never began, here now and anon, always and amen.

Echo Moth

The echo moth is calling softly, softly through the already fading summer days, its wings two petals and powdery folds, a breath and tender breeze so threadbare it's almost unbearable in its beauty, echo moth saying love is here now and always like the torn page of a poem, echo moth Doppler and dappler and spiller of bright color just after dawn or during a hot afternoon and the droning of bees abuzz with the music of so much air, echo moth light as sighing and handwritten envelope scrawled to say I miss you, I want you, *Quiero,* echo moth calling your name, my name, echo moth passing over the open mouth of someone newly dead or just fresh awakened from sleep and distilled from the verb to be, to return, to be happy once (more), echo moth a wispy carrier and refractor of trembling leaf light, a small purse of secret mercy, echo moth directly proportional to all that is good and humble in this world, an empty soup bowl and sheer pantyhose stretched out to dry after much service on a beautiful woman's legs, a mouse carrying a dandelion in her mouth from hovel to hovel, echo moth the ink and urgency of feeling, echo moth in the crust of an apple pie fresh from the oven, in the cries of lovemaking and the sweat of a job well done, the firewood cut and stacked, the garden weeded and the strawberries aglow with tiny corollas of blossom before they ululate with bursting fruit (and you can hear it going down in bright dimples of redness), what we mean when we say Thou movest me, what we mean when we say we are a church ourselves tolling with bells in our mouths the sacred hours, echo moth in the tight loops of a perfect cast, the trembling wormholes of a brook trout caught on a fly so small it's like a dust mote with wings, echo moth lighter than almost anything on earth, lighter than this piece of paper or my breath floating up into the sky, angelic for once and without undue striving or grasping or ego-clad presumptions, oh, this heartbreaking patch of staggering earth, echo moth like a wisp of smoke sent to say so much that it is so beautiful, a sprig of blossom, a light touch on your arm, your cheek, blessing your forehead, leaving its ghost trail in the sacred utterance of every new name.

Every Winter Darkness

Dark winter sky, cold dark and still with drifting clouds, dark morning, waking in the dark, all winter darkness and listening for the river far away, for the fish of my dreams to rise and flash of lateral lines, bright fish in cold clear water all the days of my life, this hour, this cold dark morning and mantra of winter and snow sculpted by wind and rounded by moan, cold dark morning and my love far away, I wake in the dark and the god within, the listening heartbeat, the cold in my fingers and listening for words and for what is beneath the words and the low hum and urgency, electromagnetic field and the mercy of a sentence that goes on forever, that is star-touched and gaining, threadbare for utterance, for the cold dark starkness holding the stars together, glistening and raw as I see the fish again and how it surges in my blood in a desperate run downstream and I go with it each time and feel the line like some bright thread holding me tightly to the wildness of this world, the world we do not deserve, the world that holds and cradles us and the dark morning sky, dark solemnity and outline of denuded branch and a drum beat sounding and I a wisp of sigh rising above the river before dawn, and the love that taps the counter with a polished spoon as some frail light fills its nimbus crown with a mouthful of greatest praise and nothing but dark morning sky and the hard patience of winter, enduring for every one of us across a windswept field and cursive of blowing snow, cold dark love letter written by the earth and sent wherever the wind will take it, torn white bird spinning and looping in the cold dark air.

Glory

Do you believe the glory has a name and do you glory it and when the glory comes upon you, does the glory shout your name and will you glory the least not and want not, the trailing vapor, the holy steam, and what will you do with the glory, what will you be inside it and is it true the glory does fey pirouettes and turns on a dime and how do you fit the glory in a suitcase, a pocket square, a wallet or purse or travel-sized container and is there liquid in the glory you have to pass through airport security—must you remove the glory's belt—and does the glory favor a particular season, snowfall in March, the hex hatch in mid-July and does the glory splash across your forehead, does the glory blind you, and does it smell of kerosene or hyacinths or hyacinths high on meth and does the glory, will the glory, can the glory lift you ever so briefly out of your own skin into another ether, another awareness and then what about the glory will take you to the threshold of gaga and how quick-moving is the glory or can it be focused like a ray of light concentrated through a mason jar, the eyebeam of a bright and penetrating valor to laser through the blade of grass or piece of paper with your name written on it in pink crayon, smudged and cartoonish the outsized letters, and does the glory become you when you don't expect it, when you bend to tie your shoes and a fresh breeze wafts across your senses, reviving and restoring you with spring or waking to the sight of a swaying tree outside the window, the branches the glory and the window the glory and does the glory whisper them, does it shade and tremble and does the glory purr, does it ramble with nonsensical praise and affection all it sweeps across, the bootmaker and the seamstress, the mighty crow and its sheen of dark deliverance in the valley of the holy salvage, shattered whiskey bottle, the pictures of missing children dot-matrixed on the wall leaving Wal-Mart, the glory bigger than the super store, the glory smaller than the button on a mouse's waistcoat and train tracks extending out all the way from Chicago to Tuscaloosa, the glory in the train calling late at night to no one, to anyone, to little listening ear diviner and refuge, its wail the glory and its echo the glory but also a forlorn agony and then end of echo though the glory is the first sound and the last, the glory is in the hearing of it and the listening, the glory of the sea in the seashell and all the foamy tides colliding, the glory is trying to say it, the glory is failing to say it, the glory in the graveyard, the glory in the For Sale sign, the glory in the lone traffic light blinking and no passing cars, the glory here and elsewhere and bottoming out on a dung hill, a fruit rind, the last time you felt cold rain sweep across your face in startling abandon, glorious and wild, glorious and uncontainable, oh, the glory of it, the glory, the burning ember and lash of spiderweb, the rotting apple core, the bright glowing letter on the nightstand saying how loved you are and why even now someone trembles far away when they say your name.

Ladybug

Little tank, little earth shell, little pocket-square diviner and humble cliffhanger in the pellucid valley of the sun, how you climb for all of us this cold bright day in January on a floor-length window surrendered almost entirely to sky, your tiny footsteps unheard in the year of the dragon or the rabbit or vast marsupial longing and will you orange for us, will you Volkswagen, your little dome and carapace containing all your insect hopes and dreams but so easy to crush between one's teeth or fingertips and how strange and intimate your own life must be within the circumference of a child's fingernail and how your shield is painted on with little dots and whorls of brightness and no oaths or shibboleths uttered by any of your kind as you move toward your mysterious errand for a new taste or color and how your life is like my life, any life as we notice and see each other wanting so much to shine or sing or pass along the blueprints of our race and do you look at the moon at night and do you pause and consider, oh, the tiny and telltale signs of your destiny—a twig, a fly, maybe a pebble that looks like you or a stone that could almost become your own hard kingdom if only you had hands to shape it and I will not touch you today or flick you down for suddenly a soft petal of tenderness for you is born in me that may even augur the birth of another flower out of these words, rising off the skin of a page and moving toward you before pulling back at last, little button and fine-moving humpty dumpty that will not be cracked or broken this day, leaving you to the thing you alone were made for, the lonely, inscrutable path you were meant to travel from one window or woodpile to the next with such intricate and fragile dignity whose secret essence might even save us from our own prodigal and windblown selves.

Mouse with Dandelion

Mouse with dandelion, mouse in miniature sackcloth and ashes and mouse with horn of so little, fearful scavenger and gnawer of beauty in its trembling mouth and may the dandelion you carried beneath your quivering whiskers this morning sustain you like a glorious sunrise and glorious sunset but light, light filling your mouth and throat and radiating out to fill your entire dark body, oh, little brother or sister as you scurried from one hiding place to another with a dandelion bigger than your head and this is what beauty must taste like, oh, humble carrier, like rays of sunlight after a long winter when you survived cold and hunger and winged or four-legged predators and now here the glory of your small life commensurate with my small life as you risked yours to gather a dandelion unto yourself and, thus arrayed, carried it into the day for yourself, for me, for the glory of all creation and how the dandelion was so surrendered in your mouth, loose limbed like a bride carried over the threshold in her husband's arms and so I sing of you and praise you, oh, mouse with dandelion, for today you have shown me valor and courage and the infinite love of beauty that takes all forms, my little furry messenger and emissary of humble beauty who could fit into the palm of my hand, and may the dandelion's rays continue to feed and sustain you past any needs of the body to the plumb bob center of your mouse soul even as the sight of you holding the dandelion sustains me now while the greater mystery lies unrevered and unacknowledged in our very midst, the same vast and sacred unknowing that would carry us all the way to the paradise of a single question mark.

The Dark Unspoken

How do the words come out of the dark, the dark unspoken, the wild sentence, and have they been hiding all this time or just waiting, waiting to be whispered or spoken by you or by me, sung by a wayside bird and does the dark give them shelter and give them little cups of water and does the dark foster their secret growth and utterance at the lips of an astonished person and are the syllables gathered and already assembled or do they fall together as one like iron filings around a magnet or separate out at mineral birth and now that the words are said should we give them silence and room to let them cool awhile like glowing embers dying down on the grey-colored slate and even allow greater space between like this   or   continue on as before for the words coming out of the dark before dawn even now are saying or want to say that the tongue they are meant for must be prepared through suffering and joy and a gift for loving mystery like any humble gardener and the words must be said or spoken only in a dear and hushed way, like this, like this and that when you and I finally learn to truly pray it will sound like a child saying thank you to the simplest things, the pouring of coffee into a dainty cup or a bright window framing the livelong day or even one's breath in one's mouth and how brief the breathing is or a slender book of poems on the table whose author is almost unknown and all the more precious for this blessed obscurity and that must be how the words deepen with meaning and beauty before the sun rises or the robins begin to sing on this cold day in spring where even the dictionary is rimmed with frost and the stars beyond listening and watching for all of us so that if we fall we will have the courage to stand again once more and look up at them as distant points of light leading the way, even if we don't know where we are going or where we have come from, even if we don't know what any of it means except that we are here for now and must somehow sing of it before we are gone.

Candle with Words

Dear love of fire and every sun and candle with words, the holy syllables that singe and purify and light the way under craggy cliffs of chin and fingerless gloves, the tender and touching kind, and how the flame is a drawn out moan from here bowing to the river and candle with words, candle after sacrifice of match and holy tinder, holy smoke, how great the love, the love and here now I enter the doorway of fire and herewith commence in holy writ candle with humming and song and pure vibrational field, candle with love and candle to light the way to bathroom, antechamber, vestibular awareness and holy throne, candle with dancing, candle with Fred Astaire leaping over the candelabra and candle with mouth, with voice, with quaking pen writing a love letter before dawn to the stars, the holy chipmunk, the trees, the horizon, oh, the mystic and the baby shrimp, holy dread, holy cow, kiss me, burn me, tell me the altar is near for candle with words, take me home to bed and wed me, oh, universe of song, of light, of Mahler composing in his summer hut, I'm ready to be your ash, your spark as we bend leaf-most to the sun, give over your mystery once more, candle with words, candle with wick and wax, blow me out and take away my drum and banjo, oh, you sweet and burning thing, you little furnace of dreamer that makes the whole day shine before sunrise.

Skin of Earth

Just these moon-stretched words and love of echoes are my yearning and my destiny, the bare branches of a linden tree or the statue of St. Francis in the garden who holds his empty hands up for all of us, for no one to let everything in, even snowflakes and shadows and the raccoon who prowls near the milkweed and the cornstalks and how home is not a place but a certain gathering of holy molecules who have finally come to be where they are in the cosmos and dusty light maternal and how I am moved most by holy verbs that also move me to hold and to cherish and bring back the language of stars and every holy becoming and the dictionary of trees on this earth as I feel their sap running inside me when I wake with the earth sprawling out to hinterland and quarry as the sun rises and the birds fly away to that love beyond windmills, beyond buildings and highways and all gentle turning with seeds in their beaks and even poems, oh, fey bookmarkers from authors who died long ago and earth and endless staring, the horizon that can never be attained, only asked for in this precious skin of earth.

Immortal Soft-Spoken

Who am I to ask of it and who am I to wonder how quietly it speaks to me, ever tenderly, this murmur near a doorknob turning, turning and almost opening and almost closing, immortal whisper and immortal soft-spoken, immortal hush and single piano key played oh so gently, oh so barely pressed and this soft note of forever, love note of great mercy, tenderness, immortal low tone and how we church for each other and how we moan and how we love what is not shouted or screamed and lighted mote of the soft-spoken, little candle in all this darkness, the soft-spoken word of courage in the looming face of terror and the soft-spoken poem, the poem barely heard but heard so deeply that it is not heard at all but you are the poem while the vowels last and the poem is speaking you, speaking me, speaking always and how immortal soft-spoken, immortal tenderness and longing and how a single scraping leaf taught me this with its creaking voice on its way to nowhere and how a letter from my aunt living alone showed me the way and how immortal soft-spoken, immortal sluice gate of the gentle song and brook over stones washed, oh, a million times and how I am washed and rinsed anew every time you speak to me from the soft rounded curves of your voice just above a whisper and how we are tone keepers in the valley of sound and sonic beloveds, every one of us, and how soft-spoken, soft reaching for one another and how this is dear in speech and person and wonder, immortal soft-spoken and immortal love reaching, reaching gently for the stars and though we may fail and though we will die this immortal soft-spoken and this immortal hushed saying and our glistening mouths aching and raw turn a sound over and roll it in our mouths for we love the taste of honey and how this soft-spoken will save and redeem the world and how it will utter our uttermost selves on our way to paradise which is opening once more with a whisper and little cry of delight, Come in, come in, you're home at last, anon, take off your shoes and dance, free to party, free to windmill, I love you.

The History of Kneeling

And how the first knees ached and cracked a little as they bent to the ground, kneecaps bare as children's faces or skulls washed clean with brine or tears and down through the ages, all the sudden and gobsmacked ones who found themselves kneeling because they had to, because they couldn't help it—kneeling in a forest, a river, street corner, in front of a firing squad, a brightly lit food aisle, prison yard, and dentist's office with yon drill a few doors down whining for its keep, all of them kneeling because something beautiful and tender broke inside them no other gesture could convey their gratitude, their agony, their Oh-my-God windblown amazing day and seed of light I carry inside, precious bud, precious blossom nothing can touch, not even graffiti or asbestos, heavy metal or a slap across the face with a studded glove and seed of light is kneeling also and how I am kneeling as I write these words and the words are kneeling and how my knees hug the carpet, hug the earth and gravity take me like a bride and I will give birth to flowerbeds and birds, the music of crickets and their holy friction circa midnight, circa dawn of a new day and where does this overwhelming hushdom come from and whence this constant O through which everything passes even my life on my knees, O, O, thank you, thank you and my skin so alive I could power a small town or city for a day or two, and would oligarchs kneel and dictators, the chairmen of many committees and all-too-serious black-robed judges as even a death sentence isn't the end, for I found myself kneeling a few hundred times and that has made all the difference as the smoke of my voice lifts through the flowering branches of the breathing trees who say it is beautiful and even miraculous to be so feeling and free.

Another Sky

Love is clear in the dark, listening for a sound, a hush, a whisper, or turning of a leaf on its way to scattering and long-ago tree and love is held close, so close its fire burns brightly in my chest out to the tips of my fingers and love is a wound that will not heal and love is the ache that accompanies it, love is a hand holding a cup of tea and love is the spoon on the counter reflecting starlight in the nimbus of its shine and love the wisps of hair across my wife's forehead in sleep and love the bandwidth of their blondeness and love outside deep in the night to early morning and love the hidden crickets chirping everlasting peace and love in the mailbox and hangdog flag wagging its redness to please take these letters, love in the unused oven and ice cubes fitted for the plunge into grape juice, vodka, and root beer and when I say love I feel it feeding me in photosynthesis and when I see love I know it is manifest spirit like roots shaping the very ground and fields beyond where my gaze can roam and sky is love in vast and glorious empyrean, apple is love in halved sections moist with sugar and water and dear in this love I walk and I wander all the days of my life and under the sign of this love, which is a many-splendored flower, and out on the highways beyond the billboards and the off ramps and orange pylons of construction love is driving across America at the speed of light and love is talking to itself in mystical code like soft static between stations and love is speed and movement and also stillness, so still and steady yet wanting to fly and love fills my mouth with juicy alacrity and love grazes my shoulder like the wing of a bird and this same brushing a holy contact and sacred offering of feather and love layeth me down in green pastures with daisies in my hair and love waketh me in the morning to stretch and work and play and these words whatever they say, whatever they speak, curve around the great bend of love's bounty and the acorn in the palm of Julian's hand in the intimate display of all there is and how love is held and cherished there, son, daughter, and little lamb on the straw of Julian's skin, waiting for another sky to lift them up to heaven.

Chanting by Breathing

A little darkness in the shadows, a little love nest made of fever, a little eclipse of leaf above a sodden newspaper in the gutter and the parenthetical hollows of a mouse hole, a little archway, a little doubt and darkness again in the corner—and what is the purpose of all this desire from my loins to my heart and back again and then, holy elevator, all the way to the cowlick of my scalp and littleness waiting there and little, little penumbra and even my private parts in the service of heaven as late after midnight hours before dawn I wait in the darkness and hear myself breathing and all things breathing, even the walls, verily you can believe it, saying little this and little that for fear that I will somehow fail in tenderness which is the greatest sin I know and what jigsaw pieces or covers of darkness I see and address because they are not alone and not forsaken but in the beginning the word spoke itself out of a darkened crater or void of black ink and sensory deprivation chamber and the world was born in a bloom and flower and though I hide my heart from others and from myself it's because my secret is a private organ counting the stars one by one as I keep chanting by breathing til breathing is done with me and the darkness of the O rounding my mouth takes me somewhere else where the light is almost blinding and I see through it as if it is a tall glass of clear, clear water asking me to drink of it with great solemnity and dearness, quenching my thirst in a moan.

Nebraska Prayer

Lord, grant me distance in grain stacks and bean fields and windswept highways where only a few cars travel, driving to unknown destinations because the drivers have lost their way and are moving for the sake of movement and because distance itself beckons them, as it beckons all of us. And Lord, help me to roam farther and farther from the reed bed to the heart of things, including my own heart, by any means necessary, even chewed-up ballpoint pen or paper airplane wing-dinging it for the radiator, which sometimes feels far away and sometimes claustrophobically close though I know this is a distortion created by my own monstrous selfishness for no heart can ever be encompassed or surrounded, only broken and expanded forever. And Lord, if it be your will and your mercy, plant sky and tree in me and the whole state of Nebraska that so many want to get through as quickly as they can. Grant me I-80 and the fields of my boyhood again and the towering thunderheads I could see from half a world away next to the wind-beaten awnings that sounded like sails far out at sea for I have come to know through much error and foolishness that all I have ever truly wanted is a vision so grand and sweeping its terminus can't be located on any map or radar screen, and however partial and imperfect this beseeching, I believe you made me for distance and no other, as things in the mirror are indeed closer than they appear and I was born falling out of the sky reaching back for the stars and how much you must love this desperation for even your only son went vertical to save the whole world and now I see that every highway is a crucifixion and every dismembered piece of roadkill an offering on the altar of an earth so pleased, Lord, allow me the seeing and contemplation of continents and time zones in the distance that keeps calling me, the one I can't stop desiring even as the stars hold their secret voices deep inside their own shining throats, letting only the vast silence between them speak your holy name.

Bird in My Mouth

Stay a while longer so that I may taste your sweet song and sing of it myself in new song made of light lifting wing and feather and bird on my tongue wanting to fly but please not yet so soon and bird perched on my teeth like a row of Cornish stones and bird the day and the dawn where I wake to find myself amazed that I am alive and that all things are alive, even woodpile and gutter, even shredded plastic bag high and adrift like a carefree spirit who has finally let go of every doubt and sadness to become sashayer and lover of air and wind wherever the light particles may take it and bird on my tongue tasting like light, like warm butter and flower and other beautiful things that want so much to sing, to say glory, glory, glory for its own sake and bird looking out from my mouth and myself a dubious tree whose fruit of knowledge has turned into apples of wonder and strawberries of glee glistening at dawn and covered with dew on beds of glowing straw and bird in my mouth our lifelong exchange only the words I love you back and forth like a tennis ball on a grass court greener than jade and this our primary communiqué that always sounds like the first time love was ever declared that must be precursor and catalyst of every flight, every soaring, every leap and gambol and the joy that makes one want to dance and jump over a bucket whatever one's age and bird on my tongue so sweet, so lovely, so perfect in every stitch and bone and the down of your feathers as intricate as the lettering inside God's notebook that contains all his thoughts and musings and all of her private endearments about the creatures she loves so much like me and like you, like the little bird, little sparrow in my mouth, like everyone, the mailman delivering junk mail and the line of laundry in my old neighbor's yard and how it fills up with a breeze as if to fly away only to hang back down in gradual surcease, the earth pulling on it to dry while a song almost, almost came out of every sleeve and towel and the dress sprinkled with bright peonies.

Blue Always

Blue always in the night in the dark in my heart and blue in this waiting, this listening and the sigh of a breeze just outside the window, blue self always a window looking into writ of stars and blue the falling-away memories of other cities, other rooms and voices louder or softer or faintly whimpering at the threshold of surrender and blue always the waking and the rising this body on loan from the dear hidden one, mysterious moving parts and the aching and the glory of turning and walking and jumping and blue the dream of water and the falling of water and its flowing north or south in a river that is always inside me and blue Tina's eyes and her dead father's and the joyous way he used to play his horn and blue always this letter, this receipt of witness you know I know we don't know is passing and must be delivered on high to an address that keeps changing ever constantly, ever wind-milling in the west and blue always this one love and this great love, foolish, foolish love trembling at the end of this utterance like a tiny brook trout in my hands, oh, the blue world in its shining and the blue world in its turning all the gentle touches and the rough handling of death and shrouds we wear to celebrate or hide ourselves from rain that always finds us in its blueness in so many drops and blue tears of weeping out of joy or sorrow, oh, thou knowest in the valley of the dry bones blue in their marrowing and blue in their matchmaking to stone and I yearn for a blueness in the falling-down dark, that place, that window of looking where I watch for a late night bird to sing for me and sing for all of us and the blueness coming out of its tiny mouth perpendicular to the stars and peninsular to water and juiciness and every insource of being that is my humble throne and kingdom to the petal of a flower, blue always in the way it opens itself to all there is, offering stamen and bud and interstitial colors so blue we can only lose ourselves in their mystery, blue ourselves and watery to the grave where we soak ourselves in earth and whisper a blue, blue prayer.

Click Here to Begin Your Ascent

And how to keep it in, keep it in when all I want to do is fly up and away until it is lover well met and lover well spent, tongue wagging a-go-go, briny palms, sweaty forehead in the joy that wants to romp and play and laugh a little, laugh a lot, weep arm in arm with St. Francis walking down the winding cobblestone streets circa now circa always with frayed ropes for belts and how hard it is to keep it in day after day, year after year through the calendar of days and the counting of days that exist only as figures while inside I feel it turning and churning like foam in the bubble line of the river and this blissful responsibility to enjoy the world and every fruit and nut of it and one day offer my own skin and bones to the river or cairn and would you Dopple me, would you Motorola and turn me inside out and upside down so that the brook trout colors can shine like dawn light and raiment of sky streaked with clouds and for this we were made, you and I, to rise as smoke to be one with the firmament and one with the lilacs who take their cues from the constellations and we will sing and we will dance and not have to keep it in anymore, oh, the moon will bathe our nakedness in pools of its own and we will love so much we will come back only as rain to water the fields and valleys and the little old Mennonite woman's garden that is already blessed because she poured her whole life into it and the deaths of her children, her favorite cat Ivan as her one blind eye stares without seeing though somehow recognizing the roundness of our drops as we fall.

Note: The line "the blissful responsibility to enjoy the world" is taken from Clarence Brown's introduction to Nadezhda Mandelstam's book *Hope Against Hope.*

Poem I've Never Heard Of

The poem I've never heard of is sounding somewhere inside me, break, break, then rhyme, rhyme, the fall colors, the autumn leaves, and beginning of cold wind reaching the stars and the poem I've never heard of is talking to me in a low whisper then groaning out loud, oh, my sweet crushed Osip, my darling Emily, and Mary stuffing rolls into her purple velour purse in a cafeteria, she so quick to get away, and the poem I've never heard of, the poem with no name, no title, no fixed point of origin exploding out of nowhere on the page, in my throat, my tongue and the roof of my mouth, scorching my lungs that must be bound for ocean, must be bound for stars, oh, holy night of shining and poem I've N.H.O., poem becoming acronym, poem lashing out with tenderness and road rage turning into melody, shouting about beauty, about love and all veriditas and every greening power, poem taking over the lily pads, the rose garden, the hollyhocks, Monet's grain stacks and Burchfield's windblown asters, the poem that seeks to fly and feel and touch, that seeks to twirl, that wants to hold hands with, oh, everyone and everything and nothing too low down or despised, even fruit rind, even organ grinder and cigarette butt and torn lottery ticket and shredded plastic bag in yon crucifixion of chain link fence, junkyard dog and spiked collar and foaming snarl, old man weeping on his porch into a mason jar of white lightning, poem I've N.H.O., poem giving mouth-to-mouth resuscitation with a little tongue to grease the way between life and death and ever after, near death experience and holy smokes, holy shit— the world really is a beautiful place and the light ever more so and poem I've never heard of holding a little craziness and outrage in the valley of noun and verb, poem refusing to stay on one line, poem refusing to be stemmed or stayed, tamed or silenced, outspoken poem and poem of whispered tenderness, poem wearing a pink taffeta dress in a parade past a pile of smoking garbage, poem that sings and says that even this is beautiful with a gun to its head, poem that does a belly flop at the wedding reception, poem that holds the yellow, withered hand of the dying, poem that saves me from myself while speaking from the best part of me wild and free and close to raving, poem saying thank you, thank you, Pablo and Jaroslav, János and Jane, poem saying it's okay to wipe your tears with newspapers and all the smeared headlines, poem that embodies the scandal of the particular and poem that runs home to the sound of the dinner bell with a dandelion in its mouth, poem that is a whimpering pup, poem that howls with the hounds, poem that sounds like a bird on the end of a branch teetering between heaven and earth and bird singing because it can, because it must, singing for all of us, singing for no one, singing because God is in its veins and this God full of full-throated wonder, poem on the verge of flight and poem rising in the air leaving a few feathers falling in its wake full of sunlight and glowing and near weightless.

What Touch I Wonder

What touch I am and what touch I wonder as I touch this paper, this page, holding a pen cantilevered to the moon and stars with poised dampness of utterance as touch goes down and touch presses gently, touch goes wildly across in galloping whorls and scratches and then I am touching all over with the grooves of my fingertips, light butterfly touch and dust-sprinkled wings and you a touch and I a touch so gentle, so tentative among the windblown branches for we are always touching the living surface of some one or some thing, a table, a chair, a book, and all my life I have been reaching out to touch some one this way, touch some one with word or skin or a string of words, yes, a phrase, a clause, a cry, a word you can hold up like a baby chick in the palm of your hand, holy name and holy writ, touch coming down through the centuries and out of the valleys and plains so naked we almost cannot bear it, and touching our eyes meet in deep gaze also, radical freefall of plunging into the ocean of another, the feral touch, feather-most and lifting, touching a stone on a mountain, touching the forehead of the dead for the last time, that marble staircase, that furrowed brow, and when we touch with our lips we make contact with sacred bolts of electricity and electromagnetic field, earth shiver and hum, kissing the ground, kissing the long-awaited letter, the magisterial graphite of a fly rod, a vintage bottle of wine and so I send this touch of words out to you, whoever you are, open letter and tractate of feeling, written touch that will maybe tremble and wobble somewhere in the universe in resounding delight and how touch comes back to me so I can touch the petals of a flower and the glass of a window and quietly say that it is good and holy to touch the wool of a peacoat or warming cradle of soup and how in a few minutes I will arise and go to touch the frail wisps of hair across Tina's sleeping face, feeling the fire and brightness there as if touching the light of countless stars come back suddenly to lead me to the first hush of the world and the opening of a new day touching all it meets in the soft pink of sudden glowing.

If I Say Grandfathers

If the first word and the last word of any poem is shadow, if the poem or essay says love a few times or invokes its timeless sense of released sighing, released raindrops, if there is a heron or a crane in it, high stepper of the most delicate kind, if I can press the northern Michigan woods to my breast again and again and again becoming hardwood myself and scent of cedar, oh, the rest of my days, if the word smug can be stricken and banished from my vocabulary and sensoria forever, if I can open the pages of a book and be quietly stunned, transported, waylaid and gobsmacked, ready to fall to my knees because of the love I am reading there, if I can hook into a nice brown and even land that arm-length stick of heartbreaking butter, if I say grandfathers again and again as I walk through the woods before dawn breathing in cool aureoles of mist, if I can know in my teeth, my nostrils, and liver that I have lived as true and hard as I could, if I can love so much my eyelids turn back to stardust and shadow and bless the windows and door frames, if I can drink vodka because there's a fire in my head and heart and the fire is called O gracious Lord horn of plenty, if I can fish with every molecule of my being down to the river in my spine, if I can cry out with passion and pain, sciatica and ecstasy, if I can make a fire on the back deck and sit among the dazzling flowers contemplating the beauty of butterflies and my own stupidity ringing somehow hopefully down through the years, delivering me so mercifully to this very moment like some tendril of leaf or flower finding itself blown to a garden rife with strawberries, if I can launch my very soul out of this poem into the very air, the very ether, if I can pray like Black Elk to the four directions and my Celtic ancestors, if I can say once and truly, Lord, make me an instrument of your beauty and truth, if I can write a few humble words to stir some one, any one to want to plant a tree or flower or wash themselves anew in a cold and clear rushing stream and thereby wash away their grief and sorrow, if alpha and omega meet in the center of my chest to make love and conceive a ten-inch brook trout, if I could touch you with these trembling fingertips with grace and grace a thousand times, if I turn and say, Halleluiah, baby, and the whole world says Hallelujah back to me, then I will know and already know that here this precious earth is blessing each one of us even now and always and that death will take us even deeper into its mystery and wonder as we learn ever more how to walk and wake in harmony with it, tending to its rivers and stones, its finches and the long grass of her beautiful and bountiful sun-drenched hair.

Dream Animal

Dream animal and holy blaze of images as I move toward my own becoming, stalking the birthplace of my shadow in a forest of listening trees who shake and sigh now and then and this becoming me also, dream animal, dream fish and bird, the water and air my deepest home, my steadfast loves and how my skin is stretched taut between them, earth and sky and somewhere a fire burning in the night as I watch it from the dark, I, the dream animal crouched and waiting, alive in myself and the world with no inner or outer but through and through and more alive than ever as I hear my own breathing, the faint insects of night, the other creatures, the owl turning his head like a lantern, the holy swivel, fierce curve of the talon's cruel strength and I am dream animal and my own claws are long and sharp and honed by many miles and many visions and I smell the page and ink and the wild, fierce words, the headlong poem as I am hungry tonight and light on my feet, so light no one hears me as I move through the darkness like a thread of smoke or mist and no one can catch or hold me, not even myself, dream animal always beyond them and beyond myself, the eagle of my flight, the mountain lion of my boundless leaps.

Fey Tenderness Once More

Little quaklings of sound, small utterances, under my breath, your breath, all breathing, comma stop then on again, whisper, whisper, fey tenderness once more, how hard it is to hold, how holy, how beautiful and the word beautiful itself trailing out to forever, to grandfather, paradise, here now and always, crickets before dawn, crickets aching for dawn, the love of rivers, swallow of coffee and how I listen as if the world depends on it and it does and it does and it does, the world and salvation in listening, in not knowing, in wonder, wonder and how the sky assumes us and thunder, drifting clouds and what to do with this love, upright or prostrate or strewn out like a spent flower and all pathways pointing true north and all pathways rife with forgiveness and little band of courage leading the way and how whatever is duty sent or suffering is finally met and overcome by flood of love and more water still flowing, flowing, and not knowing and God center the speech of all and the speech of twig, branch, blossoming pear tree fruit of life and life everywhere—especially in ink, in wine blotter, river and bubble line, poem after poem, and how I am here again before dawn listening, listening in love with the earth and the love of one woman and the single cast that would save me, oh, at least a thousand times, dear fish, dear murmur, dear sacred tear turning into river brightness yet again.

Dust Mote Deliverance

Dust motes as path and thoroughfare, a high-up awakening lighter than air traveling the earth and dust motes ringing so faintly the bells of churches go silent and dust mote a tiny orb unto itself and little lost drifter, bright in adoration, speck of the world that will float to other worlds and dust mote desiring only to be filled with light in ecstatic abandon and it is and it is and it will be above the counter at the diner downtown and dust mote behind stained glass window of Jesus hanging on the cross with arms stretched wide from horizon to horizon and bloody head cantilevered to the sky and dust mote here in this moment, this century, this little mewing lamb, and I remember dust motes from childhood when I could not tie my shoes fast enough in the basement before I joined my friends in play outside and dust mote a little Bobby, dust mote softer than sigh and like a strand of Tina's blonde hair connecting everything and dust mote an angel, a messenger, factotum whose crumpled note says "Be free" and dust mote floating even now above my coffee cup purling with steam and dust mote near the fly rod hanging above the window whose weight is dearer than a willow branch and dust mote teaching me weightlessness, forbearance, the beatitudes of light and stillness, dust mote suspended above Vermeer's grave in a soft and adoring way and how he painted stillness as a fixed and fluid point pulsing for all eternity, you know, when you read a letter by the window written by someone who loves you and the words lifting off the page in oracular outpouring to touch me, hold me, I miss you, I miss you, and I miss you, too, beloved letter writer and I will send a few motes of starlight when I can in kissed envelope sealed with my lips and dust motes will carry said letter like the light lifting above a country road after a storm in the gloaming and how good it is to be alive and how good to return to dust and all the world wandering and floating around to *pazars* in Turkey and the neat piles of dried apricots and the light spreading over them as the love I was given becomes complete in infinite particles of dust and sand tucked in a lover's sleeve somehow, the warm and salty skin, the tang of it, the miracle, oh, take me to bed or to a field of tulips nodding brightly in their many-splendored joy, flower witnesses and exemplars of such staggering beauty and the glory that's gone completely round the bend.

Confessional

I fostered the earth with my pen and a few bright strawberries, gave ink to the stars, bled a little after midnight dreaming of minnows, gave my tears to the river and my keen-most yearnings, wrote nonsensical words of blind utter passion and praise and wild abandon, got down on my knees in the garden and kissed the statue of St. Francis, stumbled around drunk and rending my clothes like a small-time prophet, held a pen over the page before dawn a thousand days in a row, hated the fluorescent lighting of office buildings and all places of official transactions, jingled loose change in my pockets, heard Tina sigh in sleep and felt her dead father's love come down out of the night to bless her commingled with my own, wrote a letter to my aunt and to my niece with a piece of charcoal, read poem after poem like a starving man whose only sustenance was verb and noun and verb turning into noun, went fishing every hour of every day with my eyes closed in the holy waters, heard my grandfather's smoke-stained voice from thirty years ago telling me to go even farther and more gently, felt myself in the middle of my life stunned by the beauty all around me and my own wantonness and lust, tied flies with outrageous materials, strands of Tina's hair, tinsel from a New Year's Eve party, a few of my own eyelashes and torn pieces of rejection slips, foam legs fashioned out of pulverized golf balls, felt rather than saw a hundred shooting stars at once, whispered unto croaking that all of it is good and all of it is sacred, whispered that I'm going now, I'm on my way, knew as if it was given by teeming eternity that to walk through any door is a kind of flying, a kind of blind utter faith with my breathing and hands like birds to guide me all the way home.

St. Francis Hearing Traffic in the Garden

And how he is patient even now, stone hands raised slightly in fey gesture of ever after and all creatures welcome, even earthworm and beetle, even skunk and slinking possum, Francis bird thirsty and full of loving forbearance in any kind of weather as he hears the traffic from a highway north of here 24/7, Francis locked in and listening for all of us, the rocking semis and cattle cars and other cages of high-speed death, Cadillacs and souped-up Chevies, oh, the doomed muscle cars with flames going down across their paneled sides and also Toyota Corollas and other means of desperate transport and how he hears and how he listens from his ground zero place in the garden, himself frozen in stone though his countenance is not hard, not adamantine but rounded by rain and wind and single-degree temperatures and his robes like a waterfall trapped in gorgeous high dive and the gentle scrolls of his sandals that once trod the earth so lightly, lightly thou wouldst not believe it and his hair shirt somewhere in an Italian closet so small, so scant it could have been used to nest a small bird singing a cappella on the verge of an earth-shattering enlightenment and Francis listening in the garden to the traffic and, by vast aural extension, late-night radio and the announcer's tired coffee voice lacquered over with cigarette smoke and national crises, will the Mets ever win the pennant woeful me and what is the meaning of terrorism, terrorism, oh, Francis can you tell us, can you hear us, listening, listening in the garden in front of the lavender and behind the strawberries and their runners reaching out to just about everywhere, everywhere, little Frankie listening to the late-night drivers as they speed away in the dark to their mysterious destinies unmoored and unhinged, high on meth with bloodshot eyes before he sees the deer's eyes at the side of the highway peering into his soul as Francis dreams of taking a step toward them but he does not and cannot for he must listen in the garden for each and every one of us, the lost and abandoned and holy lonely as the single mother starts crying above the steering wheel covered in frayed leopard design, the false fur almost purring with her sudden and overwhelming grief, the highway beneath her stretching out to kingdom come and all the exit signs blazing with the studded subtext you will not pass go and you will not ever arrive, paradise is all around.

Maybe Essay

One maybe follows another and then another, not faint-hearted or pusillanimous but the *may be* and the possibility of this sentence and at the heart of these words, this utterance, this *may be, may be* and a whole constellation of love in it and the ever wheeling stars, the *may be, may be* and may you be peaceful today, may you and I be loving and may I also be the little acorn proffered in Julian's hand, may the wainscot meet the wallpaper in loving embrace and may the rust bless the windmill, bless the harrow, bless even the defunct and no longer usable revolver (thank the little guttermouse!) and all guns rendered useless and rusty, quaint even in their inability to fire, mere relics, no guns for anyone, *may be, may be*, no bullets and no shots fired ever again, may be, may be, and may this page, these borders and margins give you hope and give you laughter, give you courage—may this page make you cry and reconnect with Ursa Major, Ursa Minor, and the least of your brothers and sisters, may you take up the torch deep within and declare I am gentle ray of sunlight come here to shine for all of you, to the light the little way, may be, may be, and the love of this possibility like the admiration I have for a woman's kneecaps below a summer dress in smooth dunes of skin and my own staggering awareness of my own mortality as the stones in the river show me the way to shining and to wholeness and the only way to be clean again, restored, renewed, my breath in water, the may be of water that holds every possibility and how *may be, may be* is walking down the very barrel of the assassin's rifle with open arms and alone and defenseless as a lily and every love in the world falling all around him, around her like golden leaves and shimmering poem, receipts at last to say how much I love you, killer, I love you bright blue sky, ring and dirge and my time is almost up, may I hand deliver this blossom to you, this petal, this imperfect love letter, this may be tattered and overflowing with feeling, bursting little love song.

Birds to Sing Me

Birds to greet me and birds to meet me, birds flying up out of the graves so many they can't be counted and birds to herald the day in sprawling project of tenderness that will not end and I a bird assembling love notes from a pile of torn envelopes for someone, for anyone, a beggar on the street or a little girl with a banged-up knee who cries into a balled-up tissue and birds to sing me and birds to give me wings and birds who do not know my name, who do not know I am here listening to them in the dark before dawn with my heart in my mouth and this same heart beating its drum made of alarum cry and clarion call to uplift and brightness and the alacrity that is love surging under my skin in the desire to sing and soar, which is any bird's deepest and dearest *raison d'être*, birds that are not my own but birds that have somehow become me in mysterious sound, trill, chirp, and warble meant to bring the world to its knees in gentle surrender by way of feathered throats hollowed out by yearning and birds to bless me, birds rapt to fly away to as yet unknown branches nodding who are nodding as if to say yes to all there is, wind, sky, and sparrow and how everything wants to sing as a bird and fly as a bird and birds down in the root cellar where dust is king and queen, helpmate and hidden lover in the mouth of a dead mouse and birds wreathed in feathers and lighter than air where they are so at home rising and falling, gliding and coasting and flying as fast as they can in the movement whose impetus and form is praise without equal anywhere in the world for the paradise birds know so well, riding updraft and invisible current that would take my breath away and give it back in the bare utterance of a threadbare root.

Pulse

The pulse in my neck, the pulse everywhere, in Cavafy's poems, in the chain mail letter of a simple plea for world peace, the pulse of the slow sap in the maple tree outside the window, tree semen, tree cum of a bark-grooved kind, the pulse beating down this very page and the fingertips that write it, oh, the pulse, the pulse, and as one scientist said, the least important function of the heart is pumping blood (but still so sacred, so cherished and grateful), all the world a pulse, a heartbeat and heart throb, *pulsus venarum*, "beating from the blood in the veins," this headlong sentence a throb, a pulse, and how the word throb fills the whole mouth, fills the wound, the womb, tongue to all corners and steady patter of blood-rain, my life a pulse, my breathing which is not mine though I claim it with my mother tongue to say what is keen-most inside me, inside of everyone, even stone and flower, even inside a terrorist's bomb, the pulse that aches, that throbs, the pulse that rages, that staggers, that lusts after and lusts for and every preposition in the kingdom of desire, the pulse of the early morning erection and the pulse of a slug crawling over a slag heap, petal pulse, pulse of living page and living book and each word shimmering image of what may be true and beautiful, what may be essential, root rot and phi slamma jamma, the come hither pulse, the goodbye pulse, the pulse inside the finger touching a lover's skin, the pulse and squeal of delight for we are made of synapses after all, the pulse of a porch swing and mid-stroke in the act of lovemaking, the gravedigger's pulse and the pulse of a fly rod between false cast and back cast, the whisper pulse, the sobbing pulse, the pulse of many nations and the pulse of a beggar on the Danube arrayed in Gypsy colors, tongue and temple pulse, and how will you feel and honor the many-splendored pulse and the pulse of a shot of vodka in this new century of mayhem and melting icecaps, martyrdom and digital madness as I pulse these very words or they pulse me, heart-blown words your cry, my cry, under the skin where the truth and mercy and mystery live holding hands in the dark of my blood, my pulse I give to you, these timpani words, this quasi-crazy poem and essay trying so hard to be it is splitting open at the seams even now as the popcorn goes wild, sunlight creeping over the page until it almost blinds me and bears and births me, love of rhythm and dance floor and marriage bed and broken church where the least of us is calling out for tenderness, for courage, calling out for love, calling out with a strangled voice pulsing with feeling and open arms ready to take in the sky, the ocean, all your precious and shattered ones, the winners and the losers arm in arm coming down the home stretch and crazed with feeling of ever after, ever willingness, ever tender more here I come and my naked breast straining for the tape, for the windblown caress and dust mote, firefly, least ash of yon towering bonfire, the spark that lights the way in this dark and tumbling world, brief beat of brightness glowing, glowing until it fades into the blackest ink of all.

Black Ink Essay

What is this black ink on the page and why do I love it so much, pitch of night and kneeling down in darkness, more than any window, any daydream and why do I feel the black ink filling me like a liquor that speaks so truly and why do I write like a bloodletting, like a flood, like pent-up release close to orgasm, soul shudder and little groan of delight and wonder but also sorrow, a stifled sob like my fist to my mouth, weathered stone that has touched and held so much and where does the black ink come from, what country, what sea, and is it the Black Sea where I went a few times as dreamer and outcast, a foreigner reading Neruda near the beach and listening to Ezan and how does the black ink summon me, how does it turn me into a one-man church with the rosary on my breath and who-what-where-when must I thank, the wind that has no figure and this breath of spirit and why is the black ink saying me and turning me into a stylus and black felt pen and why, oh why, oh why do the brush strokes feel so right, so trembling and intimate, so precious we abiding before they are gone or like a mouse scurrying in the dark to evade capture and devouring and are the words likewise scurrying, small precious rodents with quivering mouths and where may I borrow a few jolts of courage and how dark can this black ink be, darker than death or a bottomless pit or is this darkness finally a place to rest and to wonder, to surrender and be free to say what must be spoken, be written, be sung into the dark to the ones I love so the love will return, staining my fingers in black glory, black ink, and how the black ink marries and merges with the page in holy matrimony, these delicate brushstrokes keeping me from falling into the abyss which is silence, which is blank whiteness and Ahab's whale, which is terror and the holiness of not knowing but lifting my head to gaze into the sky, waiting for another trickle of black ink to save me.

Wonder

Where to put this wonder and to whom to give it, what apple-seed of spilling brightness, what hymnal and amazing grace, where to place this mouthpiece of praise in gaga mode and splendor and where to put the freshly caught brook trout, how to season his body with thyme and butter and some thunder off in the distance, a little garlic maybe, a little pain from sciatica in winter, and do I even deserve his pink flesh that goes down my gullet like holy sunrise and sundown, like the first time I swallowed my own tears and almost choked to death from laughing, and where to put this wonder again and where to release it in the no kill zone and under what glorious circumstances, stepping out of the shower after sweating in the garden or getting up from my hands and knees after falling down on the banks of a river, what amen corner, what grocery store or fruit stand off Highway 46 or any brightly lit place, what melon rind and strident cicada, what grasshopper pogoing for his life and early morning mist and rapidly deteriorating handwriting, what illegible script and scrawl, cursive and lower case letters and how to feel the wonder and coax it into utterance and gesture, whole movements of body and armies armed with handfuls of flowers and bayonets of balsa wood, popsicle sticks, little handmade figurines of ballerinas, unicorns, and something racy, little blue lacy panties maybe, smack of lipstick on yon torn napkin, or how once a long time ago a beautiful blonde stared at me while I played pool and scratched in the side pocket before she took me to her place for the first of a three-night stand and I Fred Astaire-like dancing home at 4 a.m. smelling of cigarettes and the secrets of her most private and glorious womanhood and the wonder of this, of always, of now walking in the woods with a slight hangover and a three-day beard holding a nine-foot rod and the wonder of walking to cold clean water and no human sound within earshot, cedars filling my lungs and a love so great for greenness, fern leaf, and the murmuring gladness of a trout stream, pebble strewn and vermiculation of wonder, my trembling hands changing a fly out of holiness, inner excitement and gratitude as the early morning light filters through the trees and I bow again and again to water, to this wonder, this holiness upon my forehead and deep within my breast, whispering wonder, wonder, magisterium delirious, rapt clarity and St. Wenceslaus, Elohim, and cloud of unknowing, shorn of clock-time, chronology, linear sense, and meaning, free to breathe like a bird and swoop down in the bright true air before beginning to sing like this song, oh, write me with the red rushing ink of wild strawberries on this rocking roller coaster to the ever-listening stars.

Essay Breathless in a World of Cloud and Smoke

Because he can't say it softly or sweetly enough, because the sight of it all blows him flush away, because he is ponyless, soul-dependent little tugboat survivor, masterless, clueless even, an almost holy fool, because he is naked, all adoring down to the tendons in his toes the one who sent him and wrote him even the one writing him now, essay gone wild, essay on the loose, essay freewheeling and spinning, dancing in a room by himself, because he is leaping over the sofa and leaping over the coffee table, because he is standing in front of a huge bay window looking out on a world of frost and ice, because he is in love with the tiny clipped wings of an apostrophe, because he is coming out of the closet as a drag poem and the fire hydrant is flooding the downtown streets and essay wants some free gushing water even as he is free rushing flowing stream hob-gobbling over the pebbles himself, because he was asthmatic as a child and tried to jump out a second-story window in the middle of a nightmare, because he is in love with the downy flight of swans and because he prays, *Dear Lord, grant me a grain of thy courage*, because his heart is an open highway and anyone is welcome to drive across him, even criminals, even petty bureaucrats and strung-out teenagers, because he has inherited the kingdom of noun and verb and they become tender playthings that bounce and collide and have sex with great joy, because he is root-withered starer and gawker of anything beautiful, neighborhood deer and cornfield sunset dripping like a bloody orange, because paragraphs to him are different countries with their own cuisine and folk dances, dandelion wine, because he eschews bridles and spits them out one after the other even the ones dipped in raspberry ice cream, because he is haunted by Mandelstam and his last train ride to Vladivostok, because he loves who he loves who he loves and there's a little dried blood on his best white shirt, because he refuses to be hemmed in by the covers of a book or the train tracks of a single meaning, because words are simply instruments and gateways to newer sounds and moaning, because he has found his footing in the silty and shifting bottom of a river, because when he is finally able to catch his breath he is startled to find that his breath has caught him, because he keeps asking again and again and again, Where did it all come from, who sent it and where shall I fall to my knees for the umpteenth time and who will be waiting for me when I rise again, trembling like a flame to warm you.

God-Husks

I woke from a dream and nothing to write with, not even a gnawed-on pencil or nub of charcoal, God-husks all around me, God-husks as fallen bodies and spent mollusks, broken and used-up bodies, as I whispered God-husks, God-husks, and the room smelling of recent and sleep-pellucid rain. So I said, so I whispered, so I trembled, God-husks, only God-husks and I was one of them, one of the fallen and discarded ones, a God-husk myself—and what did it feel like to know myself as a scrap-heap diviner and pale afterglow, a God-husk feeling all over for some small crumb of the glowing eternity left for him to sup on, to drink through cracked lips and broken cistern, broken flower, and all the lilting ones as another God-husk and still another taught me how to crawl my way to imperfect and implausible praise, oh, the God-husks flat everywhere and I took their fading glory into myself and wrote with my whole body and traces of DNA—I wrote with my saliva and sweat on the mirrored page and I wrote on the walls and windows and my very own skin as we are invited to do by all our flying brothers and sisters, finches, warblers, and the steadfast robins, God-husks themselves with feathers of the one true wings and flight over the burning fields and cities but also the clear, rushing water of streams and rivers who know only gladness and such clear seeing maybe we are heir to after all and the God-husks of glowing pebbles and stones at the bottom of the river as the cleanest things on earth polished by almost endless seeing revealing the only way out, which is down, down, and down-most, surrendering our God-husks to the mighty current that seeks to sweep us ever away.

Last-Minute Contributor

RV loves fly fishing loves *Cat on a Hot Tin Roof* RV loved Sister Anne Marie the only Catholic nun he ever knew who could not stop laughing RV has published nonsense in all the best waffle houses has gorgeously attempted mouth-to-mouth resuscitation with his wife Tina at least ten thousand times RV intuits the unbearable weight of the feeling world RV flosses like a motherfucker RV races back and forth in the basement before dawn hoping to learn how to fly RV uses a calculator for the simplest arithmetic even two plus two RV had an asthma attack once as a boy and tried to jump out the window RV asks God what God how God all this beauty God all this pain RV has a squirt gun whose nickname is Squirt RV calls his brother drunk and weeping with joy into the phone actual tears actual droplets that cause static but also emotional clarity whose sentiments will live forever RV talks to the dead rehearses for the dead knows the dead are watching as he walks in the river and almost trips over the sunken log RV studies his hands with a clinical detachment as he ages noting the spots beginning to form not unlike the burnt corollas of stars RV pretends to be an academic and academic-minded and wears tweed pants but at the end of the day tears off his clothes like an old testament prophet with beetles hopping out of his hair RV likes his vodka likes his vodka as if vodka were a galloping horse on some far-flung meadow and he riding said horse holding on for dear life RV is a savant at failure a Michelangelo of the wrong road though he picks daises along the way and wonders at their dripping milk RV was called a dervish once in Turkey a Midwestern American dervish who would have thunk it who would have divined it RV broke his nose and his two front teeth were knocked out and he partially tore his Achilles breaking toward the basket but is so thankful to still be able to dance to Prince circa 1985 RV asks forgiveness of rocks and stones and all the mothering trees RV is reclaiming his Celtic heritage by going wild and getting a little drunk again RV gnashes his teeth sometimes it's really frightening spills his coffee walks unaware into the waiting room at the dentist with his fly down RV is expert at losing bills RV loves his wife's hair spilled out across the pillow in the wild abandon of sleep and Danish dreams RV is alive for now and sometimes suffers from a palpable form of inner excitement that makes his voice sound high and breathless half an octave away from inhaled helium RV is waiting to put in the garden RV is a garden RV is a wastrel flower near the compost heap drenched by day with sunlight drenched by night with moonlight RV is learning how to be a kid again with the whole sky in his mouth smiling because it is almost spring and he can hear the strawberries talking to their bright red bursting colors telling them just a little longer a little longer we're almost there.

Green of Me

Green of me small rose and echo of eternity, green of me vast woods and empyrean above whirling with great majesty and the subtlest nodding agreement of a branch out to twig-most, green of me where wild animals (all of them, my brothers and sisters) go for precious water, green of me first sip and trickling of throat, green, green, green of me these mossy words, these leaf-strewn letters blossoming on this page, loving their own greenness not for their own sake but the greenness becoming itself, veriditas and every growing thing, love a greenness and birth a greenness, oh, even holy black ink a greenness and the rife praying of it this always, this ever, ever forever more and I feel the greenness becoming me, becoming you vine-embraced and vine-bewoven and every mint and clover, every love that tickles and soars and laughing, open mouth and roof of mouth and the holy speech there forming and tongue over teeth, tongue *à la* fricative and holy vowel, linguistic structures of great delicacy and softer than kiss and gentle cooing, love songs beginning at the base of my spine and will we go to a flower shop today or hasten better still to a field of wild, wilder, and wildest flowers, will we make of our day a search for the perfect bouquet (though they are all perfect and arranged in paradise) and then traffic lights the green of me, notebook pages filling with green and then more and more greenness taking over the world and growing even over the greed of men and mass graves, greening the hope and healing of this world—and every photosynthesis a prayer of healing and act of healing, a spiritual event from most high coming to us as poor erstwhile cave dwellers seeing the light for the very first time, grub worms almost be damned, photosynthesis to end all war and deflate the rapists' pricks, green moving unto thee, green unto always, greening me, greening you, growing me ever more though one day I will surely die, the green of grass, the green of trees, the green of ferns ghosting in the woods circa my fondest dream when a sudden breeze comes and plays the petals softly, so softly I lose my voice in adoration before I speak and whisper back in adoration so that no one can deny the beauty and paradise of this earth, trembling all this greenness and shadows and light, yes, holding hands as young lovers once more and then making love to each other, yes, shadows and light, showing us how to merge into one and the sigh that will go on breathing, yes, smack-dab center of continuous, ongoing forever.

How the Days

How the days are filled with passing and how they are charged with ever-changing light such as I have never known, light filling a window and light in a little girl's face after she has seen a miniature horse kick his hind legs up into the air because his racing blood dictates that his hooves must rise and soar in horse-shoe flash of brightness and how the days are filled with so many sounds and so many turnings, so many scrapings and putting on and taking off of clothes and also shouts and whispers and silent prayers that move like spokes or gyres extending out from a great mysterious center and the hub of it our hearts, our prodigal selves and how the days are filled with longing that sweeps on through the years through every opening and closing door and awnings buffeted by wind and rain, the year of the dragon and the year of aardvark and the year of little red rooster working the hardscrabble yard and little overachiever, little thimble and little trout held in one's hand before flashing back to rainbow once more and how the days move between light and shadow and season, between heat, cold, and abscessed tooth, blessed by blossom and flower and fallen leaf and how the days hold and carry the changes and how they give them a chance to breathe deep within on an inward scale called awakening, called one life here now everywhere with no ghosts of before and after and how the days are filled with bread and milk, fruit and kernel and the bountiful release of every sigh that is first word and last and the one that contains all the vast and teeming others, even gimcrack, needle, swan song, and mezzanine, how the days are like empty hallways containing every possibility, including bowling ball, cartwheel, and looming shadow, and how the days are filled with fruitcake and vodka and homemade wine made in a bathtub and how the days are filled with footsteps falling like so many direct but unfathomable statements, and how the days are filled with junk mail, with lovemaking and barley soup and how the days are maybe just one day alternating between sunlight and moonlight like heartbeats, like winks, like doleful ticks from a clock hidden in a cupboard or hidden in the gurgling streams of one's chest, clock that keeps the hours but also liberates them in shock of beauty and ear of corn that hears all the way to the horizon, the sea of sun-filled horizon, and how the days make us move out of necessity, the love of lifting and bending to pick up a child or load of laundry, the ladders of our spines bending with great humility and great prostration, the one that gives the stars their due and the moon its bare countenance of stone for all millennia and the phases that pull at a glass of water and our frail bodies, the ones we carry into the days in order to accomplish the simplest tasks, washing the dishes and taking out the trash but also running and leaping, walking and turning and every sacred gesture that includes opening a door or getting up in the middle of the night to jot down a word or phrase or nonsensical sentence or posting a letter to someone we think of often but rarely see, that bygone and wispy saint who lives far away in another state or country or who has passed from the earth altogether, the memory of his or her voice that still speaks to us with the precious authority of ever after in tones that take our hearts past the threshold to that place where every voice says I love you, where every voice says Let us speak again once more.

Grateful acknowledgment to the following journals where these pieces first appeared:

"Wild M," *Cactus Heart*
"Little Mouth," *SAND: Berlin's English Literary Journal*
"Echo Moth," *The Timberline Review*
"Every Winter Darkness," *Split Rock Review*
"Ladybug," *Animal*
"Click Here to Begin Your Ascent," *Inklette*
"Dust Mote Deliverance," *Bridge Eight*
"Confessional," *Wraparound South*
"Pulse," *The American Journal of Poetry*
"Essay Breathless in a World of Cloud and Smoke," *The Baltimore Review*
"God-Husks," *Cherry Tree*
"Last-Minute Contributor," *Duende*

"Be My Obscurity" was published by Awst Press for an essay series, and "Come Forth and Enter" was published by Vine Leaves Press

ABOUT THE AUTHOR

Robert Vivian has published two collections of meditative essays, *Cold Snap as Yearning* and *The Least Cricket of Evening*, a trilogy of novels called *The Tall Grass Trilogy*, another novel called *Water and Abandon,* and a collection of dervish essays called *Mystery My Country.* When he isn't reading or writing, he's up in the northern woods of Michigan wading in rivers and fly fishing.

Reading Robert Vivian's *Immortal Soft-Spoken* is like watching light shatter and dance across the surface of a long sinuous river in early evening—one sustained ecstatic experience in which we are thrown both out of ourselves and into a universe of connections and correspondences. These lyric eruptions borrow as much from Jonathan Edwards as Walt Whitman, Hölderlin as Hafiz, and leave us blinded, free, "surrendering our God-husks to the mighty current that seeks to sweep us ever away." In this time of cynicism, fear, and anger, what a joyful, what a necessary, gift.

—Joel Peckham, author of
Body Memory, Resisting Elegy, and *God's Bicycle*

Reading Robert Vivian's new collection of prose is like finally being allowed to be human. That is to say that these short, ecstatic pieces give one permission to swell with love, grief, anxiety, and joy. When I closed the book I felt as if I had been touched by something greater than myself, something mystical and mysterious, and I was made better for it, left happy and delirious.

—Matthew Dickman, author of
All-American Poem and *Mayakovsky's Revolver*

A ladybug, a dust mote, black ink—these are the sorts of things that Vivian hooks into just before he surrenders to the luscious language, imagery, and ALL that arrive attached to what's been "hooked." The wild swirl often starts quietly, contemplatively, but gradually the speaker (and ditto the reader) is simultaneously both subsumed by and released by that all. The joy of the dance itself seems key. So does a clear gratitude for the physical world as a window on the metaphysical, allowing "the wails and cries of ecstatic release, the whispers in what broken tenderness this is and must be." Vivian turns a generous eye, a marvelous ear, and a tender heart toward the experience of living fully in the rush of these dervish dances. These are lushly rendered proses to savor and/or devour.

—Nance Van Winckel